Introduction

'I say to you: Ask and you shall receive; seek and you will find; knock and the door will be opened to you. For everyone who asks will receive, and he who seeks will find, and the door will be opened to anyone who knocks.' (Luke 11:9–10)

NOTES ON HOW TO USE THIS BOOKLET

Try to set aside 15 minutes every day to be quiet and draw close to God. Choose a time of day when you are not too tired, and won't be interrupted. Find a place where you can be by yourself and can relax.

The 'Daily Readings' are designed to help you to read your Bible and to pray. They supplement the teaching given during the course, and are usually based on the previous week's session.

Prayer is simply being with God, and sharing ourselves with him. There is no 'correct' way to pray, but if prayer is new to you, the following comments may be helpful:

When you pray:

- Be natural with God. Tell him what you really feel, in your own words, not just what you think he wants to hear. God loves us to share ourselves with him, and our first stumbling words of prayer are as precious to him as the first words of a baby are to its parents.

- There is no need to get into a special position to pray. Some people find it helpful to kneel, but you can sit, or walk or lie down. It is important to be comfortable so that your attention can be focused on God and not on yourself.

- There are many different ways of praying:
  - ~ **Praise**: telling God how great he is and that you love him.
  - ~ **Confession**: when you know that you are in the wrong and that there has been a cloud between you and him—telling him you are sorry and asking for help to change.
  - ~ **Thanksgiving**: thanking him for others.

~ **Intercession**: asking him for those things which you and others need: don't spend too long asking for things for yourself.

~ **Silence**: simply being quiet before him and soaking up his presence.

● While it is important to have special times for prayer, we can talk to him at any time or place—at work, in the shops, even while having a bath. The more you pray, the more natural prayer will become.

● Let God speak to you through the Bible. St Augustine described the Bible as 'our letters from home'. Before you begin, ask God to help you to understand what you are reading and to hear his special message in it for you. Some of the readings in this booklet have questions for you to answer. These are to help you to understand what you are reading and to see how God's word fits your situation. This is for your use only—no one will ask to see your answers. *(The 'daily readings' are based on the* Good News Bible. *If you have a different version, you may sometimes find that different words are used from those in the questions).*

The 'chunk reading' is different from the daily readings. The Bible was not written to be read only a few verses at a time. The chunk readings are designed to help you read the Bible the same way you might read a book—several chapters at a time. This way, you get a better understanding of the whole story. Many people find this one of the most exciting and worthwhile parts of the course. Towards the end of the course you will be introduced to other ways of reading the Bible as well. If you have poor eyesight or find reading difficult, ask your course leaders if they have a tape available so that you can listen to the chunk readings instead.

If at any time you are worried about prayer or Bible reading, or have questions about things which have been said during the course, please don't hesitate to ask one of your course leaders.

Let God speak to you through other members of the course. Make a note of their names and begin to pray for them. Rejoice when the light and love of God is seen in their lives.

A MINI-GUIDE TO FINDING YOUR WAY ROUND THE BIBLE

The Bible is divided into two parts—the **Old Testament** and the **New Testament**. Each part is divided into different **books**. The books in the Old Testament come from the time before Jesus and those in the New Testament come from after the time of Jesus. Each book is divided into **chapters** and **verses**.

Finding a particular reading:

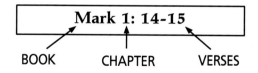

BOOK   CHAPTER   VERSES

Most of the readings in this linkwork book come from the New Testament and we tell you when they come from the Old Testament. Every Bible has an index somewhere near the front. If you are new to the Bible, this will help you to find books more quickly. *(Some books have a number before them, for example, 1 John or 2 Peter, because there are several books of the same name. Be sure you get the right one!)*

Week 1

Jesus said, 'I am come that you may have life—life in all its fullness.' (John 10:10)

CHUNK READING

Read through Mark, chapters 1–8. Try to read it through in one sitting. Keep two questions in your mind as you do so:

- What sort of a person was Jesus?
- What kind of things did he do?

DAILY READINGS

Day 1

The Bible tells us that God loves each one of us and that he wants us to know him and trust him as Father. Jesus came to show us what God is like and to make it possible for us to know him and experience his love. Read what John wrote about Jesus in John 1:10–18. *(In this passage 'the Word' is another name for Jesus.)*

Spend a few minutes thanking God for his love and asking that you may come to know him better and understand his plans for your life.

Day 2

Psalm 23 in the Old Testament tells us of one person's experience of God. What does it teach us about the Lord?

Notes
His love for us is so great

Day 3

God made us to live in harmony with himself and to experience his love. However, for many people, God seems far away. Isaiah 59:1–2 explains what has gone wrong. What effect does sin have on our lives?

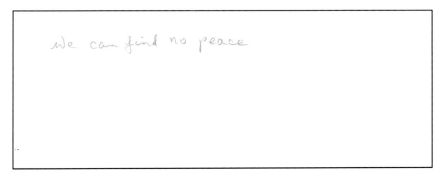

We can find no peace

Day 4

In the Old Testament, God promises his people that a time will come when he will take the initiative to deal with sin. One place where you can read this promise is Ezekiel 36:25–28. The promise was fulfilled in Jesus who, as we shall see next week, has dealt with sin and has made it possible for us to know God intimately.

Day 5

What do John 14:6 and 1 Timothy 2:5 tell us about Jesus?

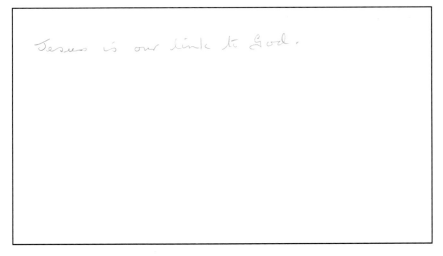

Jesus is our link to God.

This diagram may have been used in last week's session.

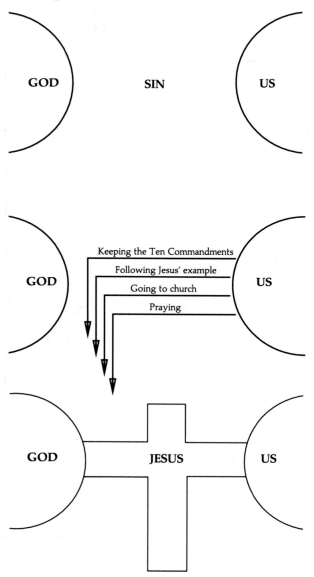

GOD   SIN   US

GOD   US

Keeping the Ten Commandments
Following Jesus' example
Going to church
Praying

GOD   JESUS   US

Thank God for sending Jesus so that we might know him.

Day 6

Jesus often told stories (*parables*) to teach people about God. In Luke 15:11–32, he tells a story about a father and his son. What do you think Jesus wants us to learn from this story?

> We can ask for forgiveness God will receive us back into his fold.

Day 7

Psalm 63:1–8 in the Old Testament speaks of one person's longing for God. What do you most long for?

Perhaps you would like to use the psalm as a prayer to express something of your longing for God?

Pray for the meeting and for all who will be there that everyone will grow in their understanding of who Jesus is and what he has done for us.

Week 2

'God showed his love for us by sending his only Son into the world, so that we might have life through him. This is what love is: it is not that we have loved God, but that he has loved us and sent his Son to be the means by which our sins are forgiven.' (1 John 4: 9–10)

CHUNK READING

Read through the rest of Mark's Gospel—chapters 9–16. Let two thoughts be in your mind:

- The people who crucified Jesus were not terrible people—but ordinary people who destroyed the perfect, innocent man.
- How much God must love us to go through that for us.

DAILY READINGS

Day 1

Writing many centuries before Jesus, the prophet Isaiah in the Old Testament foretold that the chosen servant of God would suffer for the sins of his people. Isaiah 52:13–15 and 53:1–12 is a long passage, but it contains many remarkable parallels with what actually happened to Jesus. Can you find any?'

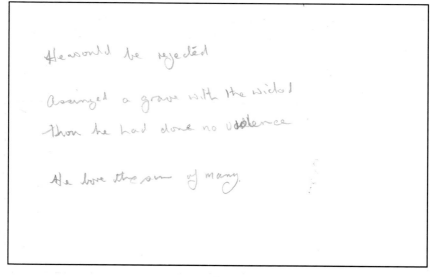

He would be rejected

Assigned a grave with the wicked

Thou he had done no violence

He bore the sin of many.

Day 2

Read Isaiah 52:13–15 and 53:1–12, the same passage as yesterday. What answers does Isaiah give to the questions:

Why did Jesus die?

What was the result of his death?

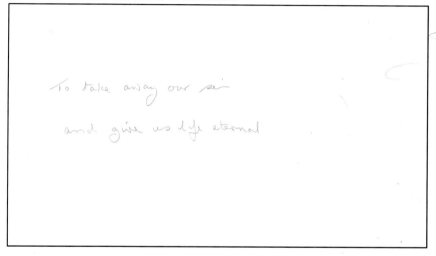

To take away our sin

and give us life eternal

Day 3

The first Christians quickly recognized that Jesus was more than just a good man. Here is Paul, writing some years after the crucifixion, stating the full grandeur of the truth about Christ. Read Colossians 1:15–22. What does this passage tell us about:

Who Jesus is?

What he has achieved for us?

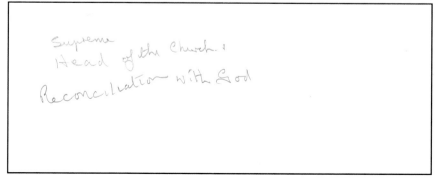

Supreme
Head of the Church!

Reconciliation with God

Day 4

On the day of Pentecost, Peter spoke to the crowds about Jesus (Acts 2:22–24, 36–39). What did he tell them to do in order to receive God's promise of forgiveness and the Holy Spirit?

Repent & be Baptised

Day 5

These four circles were used at the end of last week's session.

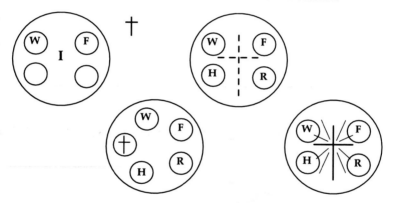

Revelation 3:20 gives us a simple picture of how Jesus is waiting for us to ask him right into the centre of our lives. These words were originally addressed to Christians whose love for Jesus has grown cold, but they are equally applicable to those who have never before asked him to be Lord of their lives. What promise does Jesus give to those who open the door?

He will come to us,
We will be with Him

Jesus never forces himself upon us but he always comes when invited.

Day 6

Read Mark 8:31–38. The first disciples found it hard to understand that Jesus' death and resurrection was all part of God's plan. Jesus goes on to say some things which we find hard to understand. What do you think is the main point of verses 34–38?

Day 7

In John 6:35–40, Jesus makes three promises to those who come to him. What are they?

1	We will never go hungry or thirsty
2	He will never turn us away
3	We will have eternal life

Pray especially today for your next session and ask that everyone may grow in their understanding of the resurrection of Jesus.

Week 3

'Let us give thanks to the God and Father of our Lord Jesus Christ! Because of his great mercy he gave us new life by raising Jesus Christ from death.' (1 Peter 1:3)

CHUNK READING

Read through the first five chapters of the Acts of the Apostles.

Acts was written by Luke as a follow up to his Gospel—you can see references to this in the first few verses of Chapter 1. It is the story of the early church, and Luke took part in much of it personally. (You can tell the parts where he is giving a first-hand account because he starts to speak of 'we' instead of 'they'.) It has been called the 'Acts of the Holy Spirit' because the account of the coming of the Holy Spirit at Pentecost is the springboard for the rest of the book.

As you read chapters 1–5 notice:

● The references to the work of the Holy Spirit among the disciples.

● The part that various miraculous happenings played in the everyday life of the Church. They were obviously regarded as fairly normal.

DAILY READINGS

Day 1

Today, you have another chance to look at part of the passage you studied in the last session. Read Luke 24:1–35 and make a note of what seem to you to be the really important things in this passage.

Day 2

Not everyone found it easy to believe that Jesus really had been raised from the dead. In fact, most of the disciples found it difficult even when their close friends said that they had seen him. You can read about one of them in John 20:24–31. What does Jesus say to Thomas which is important for us today?

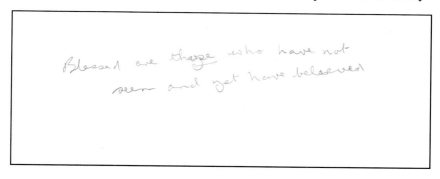

Blessed are those who have not seen and yet have believed

Day 3

In 1 Corinthians 15:1–7, Paul reminds the Christian at Corinth of three things which he says are of the greatest importance. What are they?

1	Christ died for our sins
2	That he was buried
3	That he was raised on the third day

Give thanks for these things.

Day 4

The resurrection of Jesus gives us confidence that death has been conquered and that we too will rise to a new life in Christ. The Bible does not encourage us to look for precise details, but in 1 Corinthians 15:35–38 and 42–50 Paul uses the picture of a seed to try to help his readers to understand.

Day 5

Because Jesus has been raised from the dead we can experience something of his resurrection life here and now. Sin need no longer have the power over us which it once did. God requires our cooperation if we are to be changed and to become more like Jesus in this life. In Colossians 3:1–14, Paul uses the idea of taking off one set of clothes and putting on another to show the difference between the old life and the new. Are there particular things in your life which you would like to 'take off' by the help of God?

Becoming more like Jesus does not happen overnight, although some people do experience a remarkable change when they become Christians. The only reason Paul writes in this way is because his readers are not yet perfect! The important thing is to want to change and to seek God's help in doing so.

A prayer for you to use: 'Lord change the world and begin with me.'

Day 6

Each of the gospels records that the risen Jesus, before he left his disciples, gave them a special commission. In last week's session, the group looked together at Luke 24:45–53. Look today at Matthew 28:16–20. What are his parting instructions and promises? *(You might like to compare Matthew's and Luke's versions.)*

Go and preach the Gospel to all nations

I will be with you always

Day 7

Jesus did not expect the disciples to go 'throughout the whole world and preach the gospel' unaided. He provided them with a helper *(the Holy Spirit)*. What do John 14:25–26 and John 15:26–27 teach us about the helper?

The Holy Spirit will always help be with us

He will testify and we must to

Week 4

'When the Holy Spirit comes upon you, you will be filled with power, and you will be witnesses to me in Jerusalem, in all Judea and Samaria, and to the ends of the earth.' (Acts 1:8)

CHUNK READING

Read Acts chapters 6–11. *(You might like to miss out 7:1–50, which is heavy going, if you don't know much Old Testament history.)* The church began in Jerusalem but, following the persecution that began with the death of Stephen, Christians were scattered throughout the region and to other places where there were Jews. Wherever they went they spoke of their faith in Jesus. In chapter 9, we read of the conversion of Saul of Tarsus (later known as Paul), one of the most influential Christian missionaries, teachers and leaders of all time. It was Paul who wrote many of the letters which are preserved in the New Testament. In chapters 10 and 11, we read of the conversion of Cornelius and his household. Although he was a God-fearer *(someone who worshipped at the Jewish synagogue)*, he was a Gentile. As you will see from the story, Jews and Gentiles did not normally mix, so here we have a marvellous example of the good news of Jesus leaping over racial and cultural barriers.

DAILY READINGS

Just as Jesus had promised, the Holy Spirit was poured out on the first disciples on the day of Pentecost, transforming them from a bunch of frightened men and women to bold and courageous witnesses. As we read the Acts of the Apostles, we see that same Holy Spirit continuing to fill people's lives—sometimes for the first time, sometimes filling them afresh. The first few days this week draw your attention to particular passages which you will also be reading as part of your chunk reading. As you read them, remember that the Holy Spirit still comes to people in the same way today.

Day 1

Read Acts 4:23–31. As the first Christians gathered together for prayer following the arrest of Peter and John, they are filled afresh with the Holy Spirit and go out boldly for Christ. Notice how they begin their prayer by praising God for who he is, asserting his greatness in the face of the threats against them. What do they ask God for? Are our prayers equally trusting and bold?

Speak Gods word with Boldness and power to heal and perform miracles

Day 2

In accordance with the prophecy of Acts 1:8, the gospel had spread into the area of Samaria through the preaching of Philip—and there was 'great joy in the city'. On this occasion, the new believers received the Holy Spirit through the laying on of hands. Read Acts 8:4–8, 14–17. How do you think that Philip, Peter and John were able to tell that 'the Holy Spirit had not yet come down on any of them'?

Day 3

In Acts 9:1–19, we read of the dramatic encounter between Jesus and Saul on the Damascus road. What part did Ananias play in the story?

He was Gods messenger sent to Saul.
He opened Sauls eyes &

Day 4

In Acts 10:44–48 Peter has gone to visit Cornelius. God takes the initiative and takes Peter by surprise. Notice that on this occasion the Holy Spirit was given before Cornelius had had a chance to respond to Peter's preaching or to be baptized. We must be careful not to try to programme the way in which God will work in people's lives.

Day 5

When the Holy Spirit came upon the disciples at Pentecost, he created a new kind of community—the Christian church—which is beautifully described in Acts 2:41–47. What were the distinctive features of that community?

They met together
Broke Bread & prayed.
They had everything in common.

Day 6

In Acts 13:1–5, the Holy Spirit sends Paul and Barnabus to do missionary work in Cyprus and beyond. What were the five men doing when the Spirit spoke to them? What can we learn from their response?

Worshipping in the Church and fasting

Day 7

In Romans 8, Paul teaches about the work of the Holy Spirit in the life of an individual. What does he say about this in verses 14–17 and 26–27?

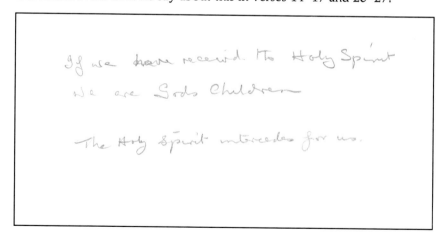

If we have received the Holy Spirit we are Gods Children

The Holy Spirit intercedes for us.

Week 5

'The Spirit's presence is shown in some way in each person for the good of all.' (1 Corinthians 12:7)

CHUNK READING

Read Acts, chapters 12–15. Chapters 13 and 14 tell of Paul's first missionary journey. In chapter 15, we read of a major disagreement between the Jewish Christians and Paul and his friends from Antioch, about whether Gentile Christians had to obey Jewish religious laws. The argument may be hard for us to understand, but a very important principle was at stake—the basis on which people became Christians (15:9–11). There is nothing necessarily wrong in Christians disagreeing with one another, providing both sides are prepared for God to teach them something new and to bring truth out of their discussions in the way that he did in Acts 15.

DAILY READINGS

Day 1

In the last session, we thought about the gifts of the Spirit mentioned by Paul in 1 Corinthians 12 and how they are rather like a Christian's tool kit. 1 Peter 4: 10–11 also refers to the gifts of the Spirit and, rather than being specific, groups them in two categories of preaching and serving. Notice that Peter, just like Paul, says that every Christian is given gifts. What do we learn from this passage about why they are given and how they are to be used?

We all have been given gifts
some to speak others to listen

20

Day 2

Paul often contrasts the character of unbridled human nature with life in the Spirit. One place where he does this is Galatians 5: 16–26. Are there any particular 'fruits of the Spirit' which you would like to see more of in your life?

Day 3

Read Luke 19:1–10. The story of Zacchaeus gives us a practical example of what it means to come to Christ and repent (*say sorry for the past and change direction*). Next week, you will have an opportunity to commit your life to Christ and to pray for the power of the Holy Spirit in your life. As part of that, you will have an opportunity to make the baptismal promises:

I turn to Christ

I repent of my sins

I renounce evil

Is there anything in particular for which you want to ask God's forgiveness?

Day 4

To have faith is to put our trust not in our ability to help ourselves, but in what Jesus has done for us by his death and resurrection. The familiar verses in John 3:16–17 remind us of this. If you have come to a point of believing in Jesus, try rewriting verse 16, putting your own name in place of the word 'everyone'.

Day 5

The most common thing which stops us from moving forward with Christ is fear. In 2 Timothy 1:7, it is described as 'timidity'. Does the fear of what other people think or of our own weaknesses mean that we are unable to be free? What positive qualities does the Holy Spirit give us?

Day 6

In Luke 11:9–13, Jesus assures his disciples that the Holy Spirit is a good gift and that he will be given to all who ask. What reason does Jesus give for this assurance?

Day 7

In John 7:37–39, Jesus gives a promise to all who are thirsty, in which he describes the Holy Spirit as 'streams of life-giving water'. What do we have to do in order to experience the Holy Spirit in this way?

Week 6

'Let us give thanks to the God and Father of our Lord Jesus Christ! For in our union with Christ he has blessed us by giving us every spiritual blessing in the heavenly world.' (Ephesians 1:3)

CHUNK READING

Chapters 16–20 of Acts record Paul's second and third missionary journeys and tell of how, despite fierce opposition, the good news of Jesus reaches through Turkey to Greece. What was it that motivated Paul and his companions in the face of so many difficulties.

DAILY READINGS

Day 1

Titus 3:4–8 reminds us of the heart of the Christian good news. God's gift of new life through Jesus in the power of the Holy Spirit is for all who truly turn to him. Some people have wonderful spiritual experiences when they surrender their lives to God, others do not. Scripture reminds us that God's character and what he has done for us in Christ are the basis of our faith, and not any feeling we might or might not have. Praise God for his free gift of new life in Christ and pray for all who received prayer at the last 'Saints Alive!' session.

Day 2

Psalm 145 in the Old Testament is a song of praise for who God is and what he has done. In verse 13, it reminds us that 'The Lord is faithful to his promises.' If you have just committed or recommitted your life to Christ, remember that he promises: 'I will never leave you; I will never abandon you.'

Perhaps you would like to write your own song of praise to God? (*Don't worry about putting it in verses or making it rhyme!*)

Day 3

In Ephesians chapter 1, Paul invites his readers to 'Give thanks to God . . . and praise his glory.' He records all that God has done in Christ. Read verses 3–8 and 13–14, and make a list of what he has done for you.

Now praise him for what he has done and pray that the truth of these things may become increasingly part of your Christian experience.

Day 4

In verses 15–23 of Ephesians chapter 1, Paul prays for his readers that they may grow in their faith. Why not pray verses 17–19 for the other members of your 'Saints Alive!' group?

Day 5

Proverbs 3: 5–8 in the Old Testament gives some wise advice for those who wish to follow God's plans for their lives. Does any part of this strike you as particularly important?

Day 6

When the Holy Spirit of truth is invited into any part of our lives, one of the first things he often does is to show up the dark places. 1 John 1: 5–2:2 reminds us what to do when we are aware of sin in our lives. What promise does God give in 1:9 and 2:2?

Day 7

If you have done your chunk reading in Acts, you will realize that being a Christian is no guarantee of an easy life. James 1:2–8 says that we ought to think ourselves fortunate when problems arise because they give us the opportunity to strengthen our faith. What difficulties have you met recently which have strengthened your faith?

Week 7

'I am the vine, and you are the branches. Whoever remains in me, and I in him, will bear much fruit; for you can do nothing without me.' (John 15: 5)

CHUNK READING

This week, the story of the early church, as recorded in the Acts of the Apostles, reaches its climax as Paul finally reaches Rome, at that time the centre of the known world. Chapters 21—28 tell of Paul's courage as he faces both legal trials and physical danger, confident that God's ultimate purposes cannot be thwarted by men.

DAILY READINGS

Day 1

If we are to grow in Christ, then there needs to be a degree of determination and persistence. What does Colossians 2:6—7 say we should do to become mature Christians?

The five things mentioned at the last session are means that God has provided to help us to keep our roots deep in Christ and to build our lives upon him.

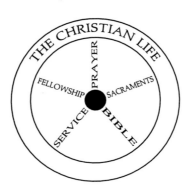

Day 2

In Luke 6:46–49, Jesus told a story about the importance of laying strong foundations for our lives. How does he say we can do this?

Day 3

Ephesians 6:10–18 describes the Christian life as a spiritual battle. Make a list of the 'armour' which God gives us.

Day 4

One of the spokes of the wheel in last week's session was the Bible. In 2 Timothy 3:14–17, Paul writes to Timothy of the importance of studying the scriptures. What does he say they are useful for?

There are many ways of reading and studying scripture other than those used on this course. Your leaders will have suggestions of books and booklets that will be able to help you continue to grow in your understanding of the Bible and to feed on God's word which comes to you through its pages. It is important that we study the scriptures together as well as on our own. Talk with your leaders about ways in which this happens in your church.

Day 5

We conclude our daily readings on the 'Saints Alive!' course by reading Romans 12 in three sections. This chapter has been described as 'guidelines for living the Christian life.'

The offering of ourselves to Christ is not a once for all decision—it needs to be renewed daily. Think carefully through the verses of Romans 12:1–2 and determine to offer your life afresh to God at the beginning of each new day. J. B. Phillips translated 'Do not conform yourselves to the standards of this world' as 'Do not allow the world to squeeze you into its mould.' What do you think this means?

Day 6

When we become a Christian, we become part of God's family: the church. Paul often uses the idea of the church as a body to remind his readers that Christians are given different gifts and that they need each other. What does he have to say about this in Romans 12:3–8?

Day 7

In the last part of Romans 12, Paul talks about the attitudes and actions which should characterize the Christian family. Read verses 9–21. Make a list of what he considers to be important and ask God to help you with things which you might find particularly difficult.

The Christian and the Church

I .... have decided
before Christ that I will seek His help to be a loyal member of
.... Church.

As a loyal member, I will:

- be regular in worship and come prepared for it

- be taking a full part in the fellowship of the Church
  - ~ in meeting for prayer
  - ~ in giving practical help
  - ~ in caring for others
  - ~ in giving regular financial support
  - ~ in making the first move to break down barriers between people
  - ~ in exercising the gifts God has given me

- be praying for members of the Church, especially those in leadership

- be prepared to accept and support the leadership, (not unthinkingly, but in maturity, recognizing the need for coordination in the body)

- be continuing to think about my faith and how it relates to my home, work, recreation an the other parts of my life (this will involve reading Christian books and discussing these things with other Christians)

- be seeking to share my faith with others (by praying for them, looking for opportunities to talk to them and bringing them into the fellowship).

Signed .... **Date** ....